THE EYES OF A MAN

*Selected Prose & Poetry
of
Dom Gabrielli*

Dom Gabrielli studied literature at Edinburgh University and prepared for his doctorate in Paris and New York. In Paris, Gabrielli's passion for French literature and thought led him to begin writing, translating, and teaching. His published work includes translations of Battaille and Leiris. In the early 1990's, he left the academic world to travel and devote himself to writing, whilst pursuing various business ventures. Gabrielli currently lives in Paris and the Salento region of Southern Italy.

Piers Faccini studied painting at the Beaux Arts in Paris between 1988 and 1990. He has been represented by Galleria Spicchi dell'Est, Rome and by Lucy B. Campbell Fine Art, London. In 1996, Faccini formed the band Charley Marlowe before embarking on a solo career in 2002 recording the critically acclaimed albums *Leave No Trace* in 2003 and *Tearing Sky* in 2006. He has also recorded soundtracks for the BBC, Channel 4, and the South Bank Show. 2009 will see the release of Piers Faccini's third album *Two Grains of Sand*.

Marcus Reichert is a painter and a poet who has also worked in film. *Displaced Person: Poetry, Pornography & Politics* (Selected Writings 1970-2005) and *Art & Ego: Marcus Reichert in Conversation with Edward Rozzo* are published by Ziggurat Books.

THE EYES OF A MAN

*Selected Prose & Poetry
of
Dom Gabrielli*

Paintings and Prints by
Piers Faccini

Foreword by
Marcus Reichert

ZIGGURAT BOOKS
International

Poetry and Prose Copyright ©2009 by Dom Gabrielli
Foreword Copyright © 2009 by Marcus Reichert
Paintings and Prints Copyright © by Piers Faccini

All rights reserved. Except for brief passages quoted in a newspaper, magazine, radio, or television program, no part of this book may be reproduced in any form or by any means, electronic or mechanical, including photocopying and recording, or by any information storage and retrieval system, without permission in writing from the Publisher.

Front cover painting: Piers Faccini, *The Prisoner* 2008
Back cover painting (detail): Piers Faccini, *Where Did You Sleep Last Night* 2003

UK office: 27 St. Quentin House, Fitzhugh Grove,
London SW18 3SE, England
Editorial office: 6 rue Argenterie,
30170 St. Hippolyte du Fort, France
Enquiries: zigguratbooks@orange.fr

Printed by Imprint Digital, Upton Pyne, Exeter

Distributed by Central Books Ltd.
99 Wallis Road, London E9 5LN, England
Tel UK: 0845 458 9911
Fax UK: 0845 459 9912
Tel International: +44 20 8525 8800
Fax International: +44 20 8525 8879
email: orders@centralbooks.com

Visit the author's website: www.domgabrielli.net

First Edition

ISBN 978-0-9561038-1-9

Contents

Dr. Gachet's Nose
Foreword by Marcus Reichert 1

ONE

Last Comment 7
Holocaust Cantata 11
Il Contadino 15
Le Perigourdin 17
The Open Space:
Lessons from Paul Celan 19
So Long Gypsy:
On the Murder of Claude Weiss 23
The Streets of Subservience:
Hommage to Aimé Césaire 27
Prawn Ravioli Soup 33
19th April 2002 36
Escape 38

TWO

Incomprehensible Heart 41
Angelic Orders 42
Artaud le Momo 43
London Town 47
The Painter 49
Kafka and The Two Eyes 51
The Writer 52
The Time Sculptor 55

Massacio:
Philosopher of the Eye 57
Michelangelo's *David* 59
Silences 61
Nomad Thought 64

THREE

Colours 77
Funeral 79
Autumn Leaves 81
Petit Poème en Français 87
A Shy Libertine 89
If You Seek a Path 103
Forms of Paradise 103
Heartbeat Still 105
Wild Palms 107
Mother 111
The Source 113
The Sun in My Heart 115

DR. GACHET'S NOSE
Foreword by Marcus Reichert

Perhaps illness isn't the best place to begin but it was due to my own physical and concurrent mental devastation and Dom Gabrielli's kindness that I came to understand much of what it is for him to be a poet. To put this sequence of events in its larger context, I met Dom through his brother Piers Faccini whose prints and paintings grace this collection of Dom's writing. We had all gathered in the summer heat to celebrate Piers' birthday, an occasion generously organised by Piers and his wife Lavinia which unfolded in their garden below the Mediterranean pines. Piers, whose music is known to many, sang and I observed the two brothers in their stillness, a stillness that paradoxically encompassed the singer's hands moving over his guitar. Although I knew Dom was a writer – we had briefly discussed the impact that Antonin Artaud had had on us both – I had no idea what he wrote or what conceivably compelled him to write. For me, there was a mysterious atmosphere of empathy and illumination in the Faccini's garden that afternoon that had undoubtedly prevailed in the family for a very long time.

Dom Gabrielli and I exchanged writing. He read a collection of my poetry and prose and commented that I was "…understandably, fighting an order of pseudo morals…" and that when I write "…everything has to be renamed, purified, words dusted down before being re-placed." I knew what he meant. His response to my particular approach was gratifyingly honest. I read a selection of his unpublished *love poems* which

I found "…wrenching, very direct, and very personal."
His poems were loaded with exquisite imagery and
pain. Could this be it? I wondered. Is it this conjunction
of unflinching realisation and unashamed expression
that has brought such an enigmatic aspect to bear on this
man's disposition as a poet, as a person who remains
quiet and calm in the midst of our world's pathetically
absurd turmoil? What else did he know that he would
refuse to say except with *written* words?

It was near the end of the next summer that I became
desperately ill. I could sleep only fitfully and so collapsed onto my bed intermittently throughout the day
and night. When I was supposedly awake I was only
awakening into a state of tremulous excitation. I steadfastly wrote and drew, often confusing the two. I sent
Dom a poem on what it occurred to me dying must be
like because I sensed he might appreciate my imploding
energy. This is what he wrote to me in reply, our correspondence to carry on throughout the night (and then for
days as I slowly came to grips with my abject state):

displaced, or rather being displaced,
we enjoy the movements in this sea between memory
and invention
hence you tug me towards you with your words
you pry open the space where we need to get lost
to find ourselves again
you document the figurative coordinates which
fall in the final understanding of the space
where naturally, and in the plainest, simplest tongue
  we must agree

When we did agree to work together to shape this collection, Dom Gabrielli's *fluidity* was the single thing I wanted most to be revealed intact. I was reminded that as an editor, beyond the rigors of articulation and refinement, I must protect the servant who is the master of his labours from the misguided intrusion of the objective observer, no matter how well-meaning the observer's criticism might be. The power and diversity of the writing that confronted me was somewhat overwhelming, but the more I persisted in finding the intellectual and spiritual source of the work the more I was aware that this poet – and it really is the job of all poets – was determined to write with his own *voice* and no one else's. The struggle to become a poet is simply that, regardless of the gift of revelation which is intrinsic to us all. To adequately express what one knows to be extraordinary is not sufficient. Not only must the poet live his life through the moment but he must also be apart from that moment. In retrospect, the poet finds the moment again or, as in Dom Gabrielli's case, the moment is lived *in* the moment as the writing itself is taking place. It is not enough to say that the moment – the revelation – is relived in the writing. Certainly, all writing is a form of illumination but we are occasionally aware of the immediacy of our own experience as the poet's words fuse with our own *experiential* thoughts. We are living the moment with the poet as we are living that moment within ourselves.

When I asked Dom how he saw this book unfolding, he wrote "...I think I would like it to oscillate between the vehement and harsh on one hand and the rather beautiful and elegant on the other, something dangerous and then something lovely, keeping the *successful* schizophrenia alive, my friend." This made good sense, but also there was the atmosphere in which the writing was conceived which we agreed should be evident throughout. For the poet, this is an aspect of the writings' character that can be nearly impossible to grasp because that atmosphere is so much a part of the act of creation. Dom Gabrielli lives in several different worlds individually and all at once, so bringing that understanding to the selection and sequence of the various texts was essential.

Dom had gone from Paris to his olive groves in Salento to oversee the harvest. He sent me images that brought his life in Italy into my room with an intoxicating poignancy. When I wrote to thank him and told him how the images made me want to be there, he replied, "You can set up your easel." I instantly recalled Artaud's deep affection for a painter who was nothing if not a poet, who lived his life through the moment, and I wrote back: "Shades of Van Gogh with eternity beckoning ceaselessly in his ears…" A few minutes later this appeared on the screen: "Peace beckoning delightfully, so much so that he feels eternity no longer eloping to far off sunsets but breathing through every pore. Nature so beautiful he does not want to leave. The locals love him and adopt him without seeming to stigmatize his difference. They teach him how to cultivate the ancient olive tree. He decides to stay. He keeps painting, death a faraway thought. There are no crows, no wheat, no sunflowers. The earth is vibrant. He develops a penchant for chiles, wild rocket and fennel. The local girls are fine dancers. He falls in love and tells Gachet to keep his nose out of his new invigorating life. The history of art had to be rewritten."

ONE

Last Comment

The Sacrifice is done. At the end of transcendence, at the end of the possibility of better worlds. Why? What sacrifice? For the work! As a good writer said: the body becoming book, or becoming painting, it's the same thing. Leaving the biological body for something different which is definitively non-biological. That's what society can't understand at all. A question of sensations. And our way of leaving biology is our particular style, if we're good enough to have one. The will is a stain left on the page by our passing bodies. The poet's honest food is tears. He senses the tug of something eternal linked to the music of another time. An image can conjure up this temporality. A good writer must live there. I am not what you see. My fingers write burnt by the third degree.

Il Professore died this morning. Of all the people I know and knew, he was probably the one who most helped me down this way of words. He took the jump. His suffering too great, he decided it was time for death to take him. He killed himself. He decided to stop eating. He had just enough strength to pull his wheelchair to the window. The wind and all his words and all his ideas tumbling to the ground. My *Professore*'s eyes closed on this life with mine regurgitating their centuries of grief. You suffered the physical consequences of bad luck. And now my eyes are stinging in retreat. There is no point speaking to me. My grief cannot be heard. My eyes communicate with dark soils. I plunge my hands down and dig at the crust. I roll about and clutch my ankles. I lie on my back and cross my legs. I outstretch my arms and press the palms up. Just as they carry you away for good now. Just as they banish your handsome face forever, closed in a wooden box. As if your memory could find a box big enough.

And now they have dug a grave for you, a cold hole in the mud. And they put a stone cave above your neck. Just like the others. Just like the others that got carried away too. The eighteen year old villager hit by a car, the mechanic with cancer, the 93 year old grandmother. Their bodies lined up under the earth, waiting for impossible affection. Just like the others, you lie in your best suit and tie. Your sun tanned face smiling at the closed vents of blackness. And whenever the passion plays, I shall seek out a landscape for my eyes to sit and weep and think of you. Why don't they feel this passion? How can they laugh and mock so easily? It is the collusive mob which you depicted so well, their sinister weakness and their eyelashes clogged up in the blood they sheepishly spill. I'll sit at the memorial and sing the optimism of eternal life which you had obtained long before you died. I can feel your cold stony hand closed around mine forever.

How do you expect me now to believe in this body, this time, this space? When we cannot tolerate being pinned down to any single spot? We are everywhere already as we come. Just as we move through the folds of memory, as fluid timeless bodies. I leave utopia. Everything I say is practical and proven by fact. I am an empiricist, a rogue to the State. Yet, we are talking of the Spirit now. What would become of us? What of our worldly memories? Of our minds? And this faith in another life? An afterlife? St. Augustin imagined himself in the company of angels, marvelling at images of a perfectly peaceful bliss. St Francis of Assissi had the certainty of an afterlife. Paradise was a just accomplishment for those who had followed the Christian way. What gave them such faith? How could they be so sure? What disturbing meditations lay in ambush for those who could not allow themselves such blind faith? What sounds, what words formed of sounds scratched across the blank tambourine of this notebook can render our intellectual turmoil as I ruminate upon such questions? I have surrendered the body.

I felt *il professore*'s spirit invade my mind and I suddenly realised how close he still was to me. I imagined his essence no longer knew the slightest boundary and could alight in all those who thought strongly of him. Thus our love for him could live and claim a long life. And simultaneously, I lamented that if no one thought of him, supposing that were so, then his spiritual existence would become ephemeral if not extinct and his newly found ubiquity would not be of the slightest use to him. In this sense, an afterlife would still be linked to this earthly existence. Indeed, he would be condemned to a vigil before his successors' memories. I imagined the afterlife was a facet of memory. I computed that if writing was the greatest exploration of memory known to man and that writing was nigh an extinct practise then humanity would soon lose any rational link to the afterlife, leaving only superstition and magic in its place, and that death as reflexion would soon die for lack of thought, and writing would follow rapidly behind, leaving spontaneous chatter and sounds to placate the anxiety of the world become mass. Here I am again, crying. The world dies, you die, I die. We are dead. Serve me a drink. I can still drink: red ruby wine. Deep black spices from the Mediterranean. Olive oil from my groves. Feel my throat sting. Chew on wild rocket and tomatoes dried by the hot summer sun. Cling to my loved ones and write poems for nobody.

Holocaust Cantata

1.

Sentences rummage through the mind,
leaves of a book ripped and torn,
seeking their leather-bound home.
Sailing parchments, green bottles
wrapped in seaweed, tossed by
the wind's current – gale force
labyrinth. Try to keep your eyes
on a wave as its myriad tongues
lick at the wood in the fire. You can't
because every flame becomes another,
as every wave retreats to become another.
No start to destruction, no end to creation.

Oh lord, where did this body go?
Oh why do I have so much pain?
Oh lord, where is my mother's hand
on my forehead?

I need loving fingers to caress my pages.
I need tears spilt, some timid gaze to alight,
to tug upon the rope and take this ravaged
wooden boat out for a sail.

2.

What it is to slip between worlds, to fall down
when you're standing straight, to drown when
you're upright in the middle of a square –
fearful of walking, like a phobia of heights,
all the people about. Fearful of being seen,

a broken down sick being. There are no wounds,
only the anxiety of going away, heartbeats speeding
for nought, arms stiffening, now having to go off
and lie down – oh, these terrible shaking fits.

What do my eyes betray?
Why do my knees give way?
My hands slip and let things drop?
My head turn, my neck ache?
To where am I slipping?
Which world am I leaving?
Which world am I entering?

I need loving fingers to caress my pages.
I need tears spilt, some timid gaze to alight,
to tug upon the rope and take this ravaged
wooden boat out for a sail.

3.

This stormy descent, which I hide from
the world of question and answer, gives
way to a strange and eerily immediate calm.
As if I'd been boxing again some rounds,
out of breath, drowned in sweat, shaking
all over, sitting down in a corner asking
myself what's happening – oh good lord,
what's happening to me?

Then all of a sudden nothing. It finishes,
it fades away. Now the unexpected lull
in the storm, quiet, a giddy happiness,
still being alive, still being able to walk
and to breathe, even if I am weak and

worried and nothing beloved can save me.

I need loving fingers to caress my pages.
I need tears spilt, some timid gaze to alight,
to tug upon the rope and take this ravaged
wooden boat out for a sail.

4.

Take my eyes from here, send them to other lands.
Take this head off of me, rip this heart out of me,
break my bones and send my carcass to the wolves.
I have no more luck now my body is broken.
I take a step, just one step, and my veins bleed panic.
I see a crowd and I wonder if I can make it to
the other side. Been broken back down from one
bright day to the next. A storm in my body,
white coats at my bedside, needle up my arm.
I forgot to tell the doctors I don't know who I am,
nor where I came from – I have no genetic structure.
Just like thin air I'm gone, I've taken off for the clouds
to lend some blue sky to the paintings in my heart.
I'm not afraid to die, because I'm already dead.

When in high seas, jump: you will hear God.
When in the desert, get lost: God will find you.
Death is only audible for death – stamp your feet,
faster, faster, throw up your last yelp from the
deep of the well. So long *amici*, I know the deep
of the well, I promise you I do. Another language,
another thought – we know it when it comes up.
We acquiesce with a stamp, a clap, a yell, even
a sob can be joyous when it comes up and sings:

I need loving fingers to caress my pages.
I need tears spilt, some timid gaze to alight,
to tug upon the rope and take this ravaged
wooden boat out for a sail.

Il Contadino

You come from a strange land, *contadino* of the south. You pull your massive shoulders across your ever changing pastures. Geckoes protect your kitchen, dogs patrol your territory like hyenas in the steppe, toads come dancing to the well, water dripping in your vegetable patches, wild olives and cactus, fennel and thyme, black snake and *lentisco*, herald the stranger. Here you are again, your two metre frame stood against the light blue evening. You were always on the prowl, every sign examined, analyzed, guns and dogs ready. You had lost sight of *cristiani* a long time ago, you claimed to be allergic. You preferred the company of your Ionian goats in the wild myrtle bush.

The villagers told me you had stolen your land, you had frightened your associates away, that I shouldn't trust you, that I shouldn't be looking into your kind sparkling eyes, that you were out to get me same way you got all the others. This brought me towards you all the more and made me inclined to like you even before your heavy hand sat upon my shoulder. I looked past your giant hands, I saw over your hundred and thirty kilo bulk. I could see some lost tenderness in the hunch of your butcher's shoulders, in the palm stretched out to a tiny frog in the parched hay.

In the deep south, they do not like ideas which inhibit profit, they do not take kindly to one who preaches against the industries of pesticides, to one who ushers hunters away from the woods and the steppe, to one who stands up in the square and heckles the corrupt and the criminal. Thirty years of organic farming and still they call you a liar, and still they convince each other it cannot work, that the earth must be stripped of weeds and the bush burnt to a cinder. They have no taste buds to love your oil, the best I ever had.

Your ideas cost you dear:
they come in hordes to steal from your farm,
they set fire to the woods and the bush,
they want to burn down your organic farm.

You went around preaching a word that daren't be heard, that the olive groves were polluted by chemicals, that the animals and flowers were dying, that soon the bees would be wiped out.

You weren't afraid to stand against the southern gangs, the ones that burn the land and build concrete nightmares, the ones that pump shit into the seas where they sell holidays, the ones that elect puppets to pass inane laws, and close their eyes on slow murder. *Contadino* of the south, where do you find your hope?

Lend us your dreams, we need them. Tell us stories of before, tell us of the way the old folk used to make their bread with wild wheat and the living mother's yeast, how olives can be stone pressed and decanted, how the old varieties of *pummuduri* reigned the peninsula before the industrialists replaced them with disease resistant clones. We need to learn about the wild plants in the bush and their therapeutic mysteries.

Can I be your ally? Let's fight this insidious enemy? *Contadino, d*o we have a chance?

Le Perigourdin

From time to time husbands sing and turn beer bottles into jokes and hurl abuse at their mothers. You are celibate and insult only the foreigner who comes to buy your land, the English with their monies. You live in the house where you were born, you will die in the selfsame spot your mother and father passed away. Your girlfriend with cancer comes and goes, you cook her ceps from your forest which you pick from beside your lakes. She weeds your parsley and looks despondently at landscapes. Months forward she will no longer see.

There are no children on your farm. You despise marriage for the power a woman has to destroy a man's will. You have the best tomatoes in the village; red and round, and a plastic roof constructed to avoid the dreaded mildew. You tend to your sheep in the fields where once your heart stopped and the helicopters came.

Now you have decided to sit still facing the rising sun over your lakes and judge the migrants with scorn as they come for better healthcare when they don't even bother to learn French. You would forgive us all for having strayed from the generous mother who deigns to bear fruit every season, but the sciences have concocted sinister molecules for the lands, for the trout waters to inhale, to kill the fresh water mussels.

Why do you invite me in with your eyes so bright and deep and your chest proud to reminisce on the times when paradise was still there in your woods and in your lakes? Your eyes go so deep, they go fetching the exact copy of an idea you formulated on a solitary stroll so many years ago before cancer took your love, and the helicopters your heartbeat, and when your eyes come back they are sad, only pride holds back ineluctable tears.

You speak to me of your illness, your heart that doesn't want to beat, your girlfriend's bones that are beginning to break. For good, for good now we talk for long minutes in silence. I seem to amuse you, to distract you. I strike you as one who has jumped the sack, a deviant gene against the industrial clone. And yet, I have bars around me too as you stare through me to the heart, because we cannot fail to see the truth: we were born that way, we will die that way.

The Open Space
Lessons from Paul Celan

1.

Last night again, the same old scene: a banal dispute. A gang jumping on their victim. Ten, twelve aggressors screaming, urging each other on, swearing at their victim, insulting him with racist words. Fists and shoe and all the angry drugged up hell of unconsciousness, the victim's head into the wall, blood everywhere, kicking him on the ground in the head and ears and nose and balls. Each blow executed with its array of spittle and language which signified far more than the victim's identity. This violence rising through them suddenly. I tried speaking, I tried explaining the poor suited fellow was already possibly dying, that there were ten of them and he was alone and drunk and probably weak but it was in vain. They were hungry for blood. Hungry to make an object pay for what they hadn't got inside themselves, these rats from hell. So they came for me too. It was blood they had come for and blood they wanted and blood they would get. I ended up bleeding too but the scene worried me far more than my wounded chin.

Paul, if you had seen them come. The way they had attacked and the insults the poor innocent victim had received. What would you have done? Other than run to the rescue? Would you have inferred like me that hatred and murder live inside them and they are constantly looking for new scapegoats to placate their basic instinct to murder? That there is never a historical moment where we can say we have been rid of this primeval urge to kill and seek out a victim to blame, a body to savage and rip apart, limb from limb. You told of the market place and the town square. You told of the pain and the horror. As they called out the names of those who had to be collected, numbered, examined, murdered. They must speak again.

2.

Are we ready to think aloud and write the story of our thinking aloud? What is writing? Is one's first book not a timid response to that question? Why writing? Why this body? Why this name? Aren't we initially writing our own surprise? A book is many moments of the question, the problem. Other writers erupt in the white pages, here and there. They are still speaking. I transgress. I take a step further past one limit and then another. I go dizzy. I am losing my control, my power, dare I say my masculine power, but in the same instance, I am adding something mysterious to myself. This passage between loss and gain opens onto a path which finally will become a book. And the book becomes a place with a name.

"With a variable key
You unlock the house in which
Drifts the snow of that left unspoken.
Always what key you choose
Depends on the blood that spurts
From your eye or your mouth or you ear."

For years I was stranded upon this path, terrorised by what I might be losing and without the courage to seize what I might gain. So I closed the writing away. Few people were allowed the key to unlock those words. I spent years wondering where things were going and where they were coming from. I was yet to discover the permanently open quest. I am looking for the space where I am finally away, where I am finally lost, where I am finally outside – outside myself in the open. The poem is this *looking for*, this search to get there. And the identity of this *looking for* is the poet's last identity. Were you the last to speak?

*Paul Celan, *With a Variable Key*, 1955

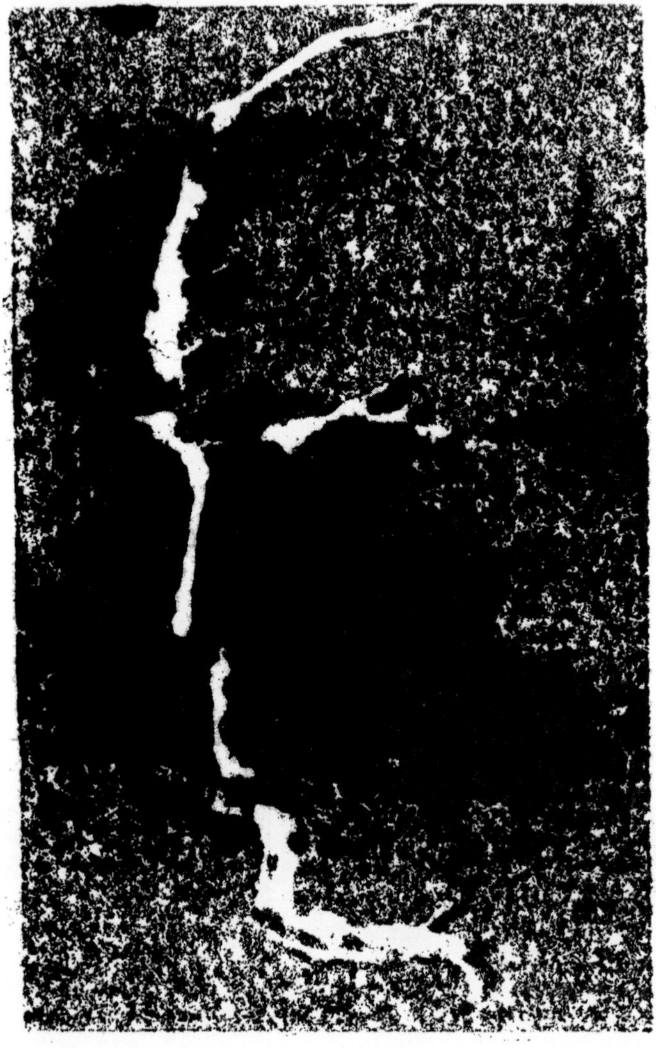

So Long Gypsy
On the Murder of Claude Weiss

We've only got words,
we've only got words in the face
of all the tyrants who kill words.
We've only got words
in the indifferent mugs
of the tyrant's silent accomplices.
We've only got words, brother.
We've only got words, sister.

To explain how you
got shot down,
to explain how a best friend
got crossed out,
how a heart got stopped
dead in a Parisian suburb –
but with our words,
can we understand how
someone pulled the trigger?
Against the murderers
of your ancestors
dragged across continents,
carted from place to place,
scorned and disgusted,
diaspora of shame,
our brothers and sisters
destroyed by the million –
what have we got now?
Words, words and a gypsy ballad,
only words against
the eternal murders.

And I am to let my body rot
in some hospital yard
whilst the bastards live on?
I say no! I say enough!
We've got to put fists
into our words,
we've got to attack
head on now,
my cousins, even if we
are the eternal victims –
with our balls bloated with ink,
with our cheekbones oiled
against their fists,
with the memory of all
our hearts full of their bullets,
with the memory of your
brains spilled by their viciousness,
with the memory of our
gullets full of their poison,
with their fists and elbows
and kneecaps splitting
our temples and lips,
with the memory of all
their flames and cinders.

I'll put a knee in
their belly of murder,
I'll venture an elbow into
their cosy eyes of satisfaction,
I'll venture some spittle at
their humiliating grins
and snickering,
I'll venture to break my fists
on their sinister technology,

I'll come down in a storm
and blow the whole sham
to smithereens.

Yes, I'll place fists
in my words,
I'll deliver
the decisive blow.

To murder murder.

The Streets of Subservience
Hommage to Aimé Césaire

1.

Inside me, the other speaks, aches in the present time. I see my corpse faraway upon a sundrenched beach, I see it faraway in the ravines of unconsciousness. My island is unreachable, it is haunted by me. Infectious feats and time-honoured boredom quartets: the expansive plains of conquest's eye rot and disgrace their very own visions. Oh, imperial wreck and foul stench of decay!

They don't heed easily, catastrophe can be piled upon catastrophe. Yes, and despite our fine common sense, death deeds pursue their bloody path, their clever follies heed only imminent danger. And when uncovered, they just have a quick change of mask, these grey gentlemen of charts and telescope. Unlike these mouldy heads, I preach nothing. Stay still awhile and hear yourself breathe. Why go conquering when conquering is in vain? But such negativity does not fare so well with these humanitarians of the right and just coinage. They prefer profit to war, but hark the news is out: war is a form of profit, and how little profit margins dilly-dally when in search of new metamorphoses!

And if one tiny bean should be seen
to jump out of the sack,
how now this inconsequential seaman
must be brought back to reason.

But you ask me who is speaking here, a child of eleven sole years? That kid who never smiles and never says a word in class. I do not speak, dear sirs, it is the insane root your immense idiocy forced me to imbibe as if medicine. It speaks alone despite me, but I perceive all your truth as lies. Gentlemen, forgive my criminal intelligence. I hurry away now into the murky metropolis. I fall with tumbling mind into another freedom. You will punish me for the sin of reason alone.

Repetitive tugs and knocks wish to construct an ego, a being forged by the cruelty of the master. But why impose a vision of expansion, why place a tree in my head and say yes or no, why show me a straight line and say ready steady go, why pose problems with only one solution, why ask when I cannot ask why you ask? No, there is a sea inside me which refuses this nonsense!

I prefer the gypsy guitarist
to the judge and the officer.
Sing on gypsy! There was sea
and to sea we shall return!
Roll on carriage! Which bank
shall we rob today?

And she who they fear, she who lives by the river, I have made her my ally. My whole body is slack-bellied scales, and my venom nurtures her potions. Nothing ever dies, everything comes around. You taught me that the river is infinite, and you never leave the river. Oh sweet invisible footsteps, all reverses where I sit, all coordinates are swept up by the river, all the dreams, the realities, the truths. Ah joyous destruction!

Humour is the thing humanity has the most difficulty understanding. Witch, come along and suck my marrow, take my bone and make it sing, unscrew the nail and upon the poetic oceans make it sail. Yes, give the earth a spasm and your heart will skip a beat. Now gather the words and spill them among the dwindling numbers of our maiden friends. Giants in small carcasses, we are invisible. Eternally migrating swallows, we are as mosaics under a million shades of light.

So we are never born when born,
we are unborn at birth,
we await the vampire's bite.
Thus madness is a form of reason
and reason is as vulnerable as
the non-born is the new-born.

2.

Sometimes I am all wound with adders who with cloven tongues do hiss me into madness. I abandon myself to hellfire. Better than this cancerous swill of lipless condescension. I close my hand, and my fist grows about my hand. I have no friends, I have become one with the earth and her spirits have received me into their dens and dungeons. I am crevice and I am tree. I am wind and I am serpent. I predict your downfall from the bubbles in my boiling veins. Too long have I accepted your lies as my own, too long have I inherited from a generation hideous with hypocrisy, too long have I heard the small preach superiority, too long have I suffered these bitches pregnant with bigotry, too long have they made me kneel and say *yes* to boredom's truth. I suppose I should say *yes* just like the braying masses, I should say that we live in the most happy of times and nothing could be better and humanity has never done more than await this progressive era. I suppose I should, and maybe I will. Perhaps I'll join the eternal slave trade. But I don't intend to grow up just yet, not to uphold a system of infinite oppression.

Our laughter is so impossible it becomes uncontrollable. And when we use words, they are like poisoned darts and bloody splinters. As real as words have ever been! And even the bluesman and the gypsy guitarist will look up from their beautiful cruel labours. But my words say this: I am not the colour of snow and I shall mount guard before no prison. There's only one thing that turns you mad: self-evidence of the truth. Do you hear me schoolmasters? There is a cunt lurking in every triangle and a prick up the arse of every generality. There are oceans of semen in every complex, Oedipus is an eye afraid of the truth in holes. Last night, I plucked out *my* eye and stuck it in her hole.

I hustle and the grass is my bustle, all around me are fossils. Business ain't so good. In the fine greying grass, I slide and cuss. Should I confess now? Certainly. Find the priest who won't faint at what I tell him. Let him pray for I sing under torture. All your clamped stiff-jacket conspiracies, your enforced silences, your *postiche* dress codes and *panopticon* million eyes in the final analysis make me laugh, make me laugh away from the path, high up in the sky. I strayed from the path and found nothing but joy. No, fear is not my companion. My fear is of the impotent, the criminals who sleep to hide their crimes. Ashen by those great playing fields, I walk blind. Next the pasturelands green, I walk blind. Impenetrable and indifferent, I smile mystery.

Time to vomit it up, this great theatre of the grotesque. Time to vomit up this endless drone: mommy/daddy, wad size, car size, dick size. Time to vomit up the great ladder worshippers, the great matrix accent job school haircut too. Time to release the bile of centuries, surveillance strategies, pristine order, small print, bottomless souls! Time to send the *cathedral* crashing, along with the *great mirror* of the world! Yes, rent the glass tinted mould, send the *truth* to the desert to find its master! I have seen through you, I have cried too many tears on your account. And now, everywhere I tread I find peace. As I walk, the trees amble quietly along beside me. These long eyes shall lay themselves down upon your sweet charms, oh lady of the night, for these rantings are done. I am expended, the streets of subservience are no more.

Prawn Ravioli Soup

Buttoned down in the park, lying bare-chested on the dry bench, the narrator memorizes Holderlin aloud: *'We are a sign that is not read. We feel no pain, we almost have lost our tongue in foreign lands.'* He looks up from his notepad and humans seem no more than robots or, at best, animals. They move about in hereditary poses. Their exaggerated unconsciousness gives them a strictly unreal aura. The words that speak from the page seem more real than these humans of flesh and bone. Time passes. The thought sinks in until Socrates reminds the dreamy writer of the ancient and indelible values of humanity: *'Who the deepest has thought, loves what is most alive, who has looked at the world, understands, youth at its height, and wise men in the end often incline to beauty.'* So being different is a form of paradise after all. The senses are left to roam, the pen is here to bring them back together again.

Head fills as it absorbs foreign accents. The road to the Chinese takes us through the red light district. By accident? Does the narrator know where he is going? Feeling of looseness in the head. Head empties. Cars raise the volume of the passing accents. *Drifting again.* Laugh with the busty grannies waving their handbags on the pavements. Lick your lips granny. *Me? No, I'm going for a Chinese thank you.* Middle-aged ladies offering their arses like the salesman his leather coats. *Wander laugh ramble.* Flashy lights indicate video projection booths. Gentlemen hurry in and out as if to catch a train. Others pretend not to notice. A Chinese girl sniggers. Large simulacra of penises are presented to the passerby.

The guy says: 'Really good dirty videos here. Real filth! Cheap prices! Bargains!' A group of skinheads charges out from one of the flashing shop fronts: 'Did you see the size of that guy's dick?'

Soupe de raviolis aux crevettes monsieur je vous prie oui thé jasmin c'est tout oui oui... This is what he came for, the most fantastic Chinese in Paris. Shrimp, lettuce, spring onion, chili sauce. From quartier to quartier, from language to language, from city to city, from music to music, still Holderlin stays. We remain unread. Are we any further in understanding the being of becoming? How old are we when we become? Can we not become ageless? Thus old can we not grow young?

He writes as he sips his soup:

These are not my words. I borrowed them. I drifted down the street. I followed one accent, one face. I tried to understand the church. What meaning was left, having confession? – as the pornographic world seems to take hold more every day. I observe their movements, their body language is unequivocal. At the same time as they are showing everything, their traumas are being hidden. A new type of consensus grows where every lapsus is controlled, where signs are paramount. So how can they express their fear, their weakness? Surely they cannot love this pornography world? I hear them as I pass them in the streets. I overhear them as they lose control. I write everything down. I want to describe in notations this passage in and out of streets, rooms, pages. This new multiple consciousness.

The young writer has his head lowered over his *cahier* and his hand scribbles at the tiny squares. City life carries on unperturbed. Nothing perturbs a city, least of all writing. Life is not elsewhere but here in the street where we are all strangers somehow. You can see *wandering* in their eyes. They lean on fences and gates and walls and send verbal missiles through exhaust fumes and *ganja*. This African gentleman screaming: "You understand, Madame, I've been a tourist here in Paris for the last nine years."

There is no transcendental point from which culture can be judged. We have to dive in. *Coriander Garlic Lemongrass Chili Chicken Broth Prawn Wun Tun Noodles Spring Onion.* In mid-sentence. We have to dive down into the blindfold sentence of difference.

He writes:

To think in affects. Knowledge is a trap to send you to Culture School. To teach you the history of transcendence. We do not think of ourselves as having existences but rather we feel ourselves to be full of affects. We do not laugh at failures. We do not criticize from the point of view of knowledge of our culture and from its supposed lack in others because we forget as much as we remember. This is what enables us to sing. A rebel is someone who says yes to saying no! Anarchy. Think of Léo Ferré on all fours imitating a dog. Anything better than being a human! We present a challenge to the female clan, an enigma, a problem, a wonky equation: can there be a lesbian man?

As adolescents, we look for the truth to dislodge the father. To write is a patricide, an attempted coup on the fatherland via his darling madre lingua. Early on we sense that mummy has control, we also sense that our patricide is merely a camouflage for some far more perturbing attack on mummy via her lingo. A writer is a matricidal fool on the rampage. He must seek perpetual movement to sustain his words. He must find a no man's land where he can be as unknown as a tramp. For he must camouflage his efforts, his secret attempt to bugger her lingo just as he encourages freedom to emerge, fate to shine, beauty to rise from the ashes. What comes must come and when it comes we must be ready to harvest.

19th April 2002

Out of the horizon of speechlessness,
my hands cannot touch your words,
I haven't the heart to hunt you from my dreams.
Whose eyes cried last night when they killed our sister,
was it your dream or was it mine of you?

I sat with a man,
I asked him why he had to kill,
I asked him questions no man can answer.
I write from asking questions without answers,
futility's words upon the lime tree's bough.
I sit here as blossoms float down onto the page.

Why did you have to lie with the killer man,
or was it the dream of death which bewitched you?
Your hands were big enough to cover your eyes.
Enough alcohol to lie,
enough to kill a brother and a sister,
two less in a family that never was that large.

How many footsteps to this door,
how many pink petals fall before I get here,
how many words make a poem?
More certainly than the energy in the hand
round my gentle sister's jugular.

You left before living,
you hoped before hope had meaning,
you held his hand.
You should have been able to look into his eyes,
you should have been able to read his grin,
but they hadn't taught you that at school.

I creep around amidst the trees,
I look at the wind for hours,
I see the sun burst over the hills.
Tears can't reach up to the blue,
nor can I drink from the sun,
all the noise raining down
like a blanket over these flames
which cry out for the nameless.

Escape

I can escape you who are speaking through me.
I can escape you who are pursuing me.
I can escape you who love me.
I can escape myself who is dying.
I can escape myself by becoming one with death.
Death is an ocean of forgetting.

I shall meld back into the silence
from which I was falsely brought out.
I shall disappear back into absence,
into an unknown ocean.
Dreams of crashing waves
shall remember me as they eradicate
the sands of my writing.

TWO

Incomprehensible Heart

Incomprehensible heart, speak to the white clouds. Heart, find the means to meditate finally, alone in this strange landscape. My eyes close on the hectic threats and the hysterics. I'm at one with this body which speaks. There are several bodies in here; each lives in its own time, as if the metaphysical written dimension were a different way of feeling time. Here fall peaceful words. On other occasions, you might say these are a madman's words. Yes, but they are not spoken by the same person. They are lived in a landscape. They drift down on a torrent. They burst forth from a storm cloud. My life is a succession of landscapes. I am consequently tree, grass and rapids, although I have not witnessed rain in months. The sun is burning, my darkness my protection.

The poets had imitated the mad and the ostracised. They had fallen purposefully from their class and race. Their revolt had gone hand in hand with their banishment. Or had they not written to follow this route, to be allowed to transform their bodies in this way, their faces, their voices, their clothes and their language? But now that route is barred. The outside has been hunted down, derided and falsified. And yet the poets' revolt still exists. Yes. So why can we no longer imitate? Because we must imitate from the inside. We must hide away during the phases of revolt and reappear when our journey has ended, imperceptibly like the grass. We must go from one point to another with miraculous speed. Yes, but how when we are nobody, when we are movement itself?

Angelic Orders

The thread is in your head. You lie down, close your eyes, the sentences write themselves one by one. The block of sentences is ready. You get up to write these new thoughts down, and yet the path from the bed to your desk is enough for you to lose the thread. But a sense of it remains. Different words. The overall meaning remains intact, although the initial perfection is lost. One word omitted is enough to lose the beauty. The following is a remnant of such a *perfect* lost book.

Imagine an ocean, waves like voices on the silent beach, the poet imperceptible amidst the seahorses, amongst the angelic orders. Have we become stone to the sound, scalded by the sun, incapable of joining with the echo?

Artaud le Momo

Since I began to read him again, I have the humour of an assassin. No other writer makes my blood boil with fever, sending dark looks of silver steel through the brains of ordinary lambs. I am afar on the rafts of invective. I have loosened the final knot of inhibition. He is pulling me. Rest assured I must come back. His country is parched and pale like ours. His black sun shines and brings the desert in an instant. There are snakes too rustling through the fires. His stars at night are paintings. His moon and its eclipse call to us. They are poetry. All I need do is open my lips to the cool northern wind. He is calling me again. All these years hence. His suffering like a second skin. I say to myself: thank goodness they refused his poems! Thank goodness they told him he couldn't write! Thank the Lord they said he couldn't think!

•

You come asking for me. You come looking for me. You come touching my skin. You come asking me questions I cannot answer. You come looking for me when I am not here at all. You come feeling with your hands when I have lost all attributions. You come seeking one who has taken flight.

It is in the little things that love grows. In the smiles that pitch happiness on a wall. In the sentences we write on napkins and tablecloths. In the songs we invent at midnight for the sole echo of a star's approbation. In the kisses a newborn blows through his laughter at dawn.

•

Power had no hold upon him, still less the medicine he loathed and its paltry knowledge of the body's capacity. The doctors didn't understand a word he was saying because they never listened. They just consulted books and compared pictures. They diagnosed him with a thousand ills but the deep pounding passion in his body, the miraculous feed of paints and lines and sounds, this, they could never diagnose. They claimed it was some excrescence of a rotten organ. They could not imagine that he had been robbed of his beauty, that he had been extracted from his true being and dumped into a rotten, senile world. They could not see the poetry in his hatred. They had studied hard but could not read. They had studied too hard and become short sighted and hard of hearing. They had learnt to count and read graphs but had forgot how to look for beauty. So the world of beauty closed itself off to them. They didn't know how to laugh, couldn't admit how ludicrous they were, these jailors of the soul. They had no training in how to give birth to their tiresome mothers or how to invert maternal and grand-maternal influence into laughter. How then could you expect this apprentice sorcerer, Artaud le Momo, to trust them?

He could howl and bite all he liked, there was no contest. The white coats outnumbered him. As they encircled him with their organ measuring brains, they had everything but he had nothing. They stripped him of all he had down to his very mind, till he had no mind left. They left him there with oceanic breath shouting in his veins. And all the spells his avenging mind could concoct to keep the *psychos* at bay proved in vain. How many exercises must one learn to protect oneself from this putrid stinking disease called society? Life, as they call it, being a form of contagious bug , no reasonable soul would ever wish to be pushed into it – nor death, for that matter, which they use as a means of keeping the mass in tow.

•

You come again and again and I hug your every breath with hope. You must keep looking until you find me. You must not give up. I am not far away. I do not care to swim away to sea. I prefer the rocks and the bushes, the fig trees and the olives, the cactuses and the lizards, these ancient stones where the Greeks sat. I am sorry I do not like pets. I do not like cats nor dogs. I have no sympathy for tears. I prefer to follow the snakes across the rocky plains. I prefer to sit in the Mediterranean bush and inhale pungent aromas. I may seem angry. I may glare into the open spaces but I am on a journey, way out there, with the greatest poet. I am in the land of the Tarahumara.

•

He believed ferociously, and how great his disappointment must have been to see the traitors and the pariahs, the liars and the cheats ruin his every initiative – their derisory scorn, hand in hand with their medicine. Lets give him the treatment, they intone. We'll teach him the straight and narrow, they declare. The asylum gates slammed shut. Nine long years of electro-shock treatment in the stench of mad folks' faeces, drinking down his inmate's piss, his body slowly eaten away, his bones bashed, his teeth eroded, his anus devoured by cancer.

And still the indomitable breath of words came, and still he wrote, and still he strived for beauty, and still he recited his heart's hopes and collected his thoughts in volumes of infinite ledgers. Saint Antonin of Parigi, Turkish Gypsy from the middle ages, father of your grand mothers, fearless son from beyond the history of names, lend us some light, strike up some hope from the dark caves, make us laugh again, make us roll around on the floor in stitches, teach us to love again, teach us to see again, teach us to breathe again.

•

I am coming back now with fire in my lungs. I am running on the rocks overlooking the Adriatic seas from Albania. I have been away a long time I know but I have poems in my pockets. I have figs and I have fennel. I have the scent of thyme and the taste of wild rosemary on my lips. I have my hands stained with black olive. I have convinced the stars to expand the principles of mystery. I have been running for days and nights. I have mated with freedom.

I am waiting for you.
You are the gift.

London Town

You've got to make a start somewhere – a lunge in the dark. This is where I find you, ambling along with your paintings on your shoulder, evening parks on your canvas. Something always glows, a lamppost or your love's eyes. Green grass turned black in the garden tonight. The tall buildings are indifferent to our suffering. Our love pines. Painting is a desperate jump into a black hole, a place where you can find yourself in the company of past gods – the god of black grass, the spirit of freed leaves, the curse of winter when summer never comes. I see you walking through your canvases. How you swagger, mister shadow! I imagine it's pretty cold over there in that city, that to paint such images you have to wrap up warm – clap your hands and stamp your feet, keep your eyes open there could be snow on the way! Television is the never-ending invasion. Your scenes have no trace of this idiocy. They are blank, the stare of oblivion has turned day into night. There are no bombs, no dead, no blood, no sex, no smiles, just the distension of light as it becomes dark and turns hell into purgatorial evensong.

The Painter

The painter is banished from the harbour of the *self* by his own destructive will. He sets on a journey where he lets his mind bounce off the wall and he catches the rebounding sounds which signal new territories of expression. When he comes back in with that dangerous sinner's smile, he'll need years of work in order to present his excuses to the world for being *different* but when he does the irony will be complete and with a swipe of laughing unease.

The painter is frustrated because he feels he is being asked to be an entertainer. He does not wish to paint the image of an image as this world is nothing but that. He hates entertainment in his gut. But there's something theatrical in the painter's auto-portraits. This *unreal* aspect hints at the humour he might find in what his critics might say about what he *didn't* intend. Death is the painter's neighbour, he paints a living body as a corpse. He traces time with his brush knowing the damage he can do. He takes the crust *and* the shine off the dentition of existence. His paintings have begun to draw circles, his whole life has become a mobile larva of mental energy.

It would be interesting to ask the painter about the temporality of his painting. Whether from one painting to the next there is an abrupt break or whether (as in writing) each day follows on from the previous one as if the painting itself were enveloped in its own very specific temporality. Painting by virtue of its visibility causes problems, especially for the painter. This is why the environment in which he paints is so crucial. Van Gogh suffered for constantly being spied on. Picasso chose to put himself on a stage. Bacon used disorder as a means of camouflaging his intentions – his paintings *seem* to emerge from chaos.

The painter tells me:

I am looking for the souls of all people but some souls remain on the surface of the picture. I am striving, I don't want to paint masks. I see spiteful masks everywhere. I am afraid of the mob and I see the mob's mask everywhere. The mob seeks out its victims. For most people, painting must either be decoration or have some social use. In the face of the mob, I masquerade as an artisan, a craftsman, a hard-worker at the easel. Only this way do I avoid punches down at the pub. What if I told them the best work comes from dreams or idle walks by the sea? You have to save a little piece of mob in yourself to stop yourself from being carved up uselessly. It's true that all this brings on a terrible sadness, it's difficult to explain. There's a deep melancholy – from soul to soul – that I stretch across my canvas. One day, they will call it a landscape of wandering souls.

Kafka and The Two Eyes

Dear Kafka, you had one eye larger than the other, the left one. The impression one has when looking at you is of a different intensity, a difference so huge we infer a schism in the soul, as if you had been given one eye from one person and one eye from another. Some of us are like this. You knew only too well that every word employed by the writer can turn against him. Perhaps it is this cruel inevitability that gives us two different eyes.

The Writer

Edmond Jabbes, the Egyptian Jew, seems to me to be the writer who has come closest to giving writing back to its real dimension, of eliminating false images. He writes: *Tu écris les yeux baissés, mais le ciel est dans tes yeux.*

I still dream of this other kind of book, but I've fallen by the wayside. I sleep while soldiers wade through blood and the stink of death. I'm angry. Some say writing should tell a story – it should describe something – when it is rather a cutting away at the sores of life, a pummelling away at the enemies of existence. It is a path toward silence, an experience beyond any kind of limit. And it is a war of attrition to get to this place but once there, the writer feels a strange sense of belonging, a clandestine hierarchy of angels! Do you not hear our voices? They insist on calling it *non-sense* when our voices are the very basis of future sense!

I write from the gutter, from an evacuation point in the streets. This is where I find some truth. Truth is still a useful concept to me. I wander the streets as a shadow and examine expressions. I try to find the face of a drug addict, a murderer, the grimace of desperation. I draw poems from hidden treaties. I have to enter into conversation even if my characters never existed. I spend longer with books than people.

I speak of writers as if they are still writing. It's the book of books which is constantly being re-written. Do you think we could go back in time to the previous ones, the unpretentious ones who chose secrecy and vowed to wait for their hour? Do you think we could choose to be the secret poets ready to disappear to protect the beauty of their work?

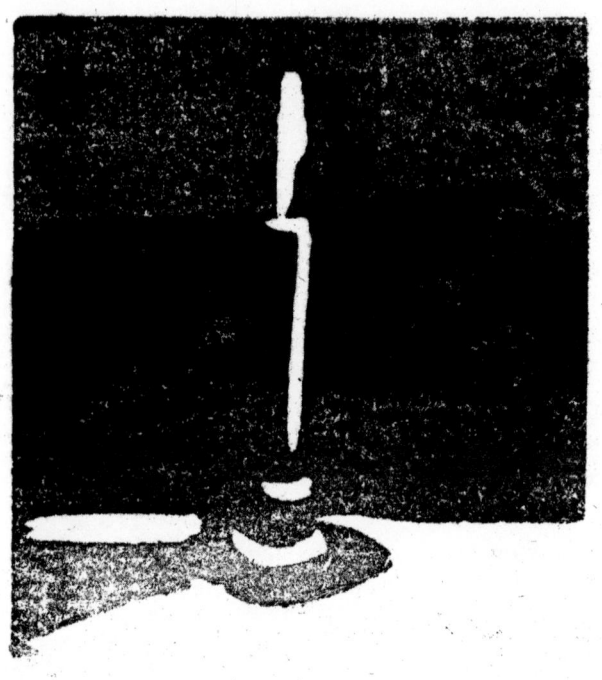

The Time Sculptor

I write these ideas down, sculpting the contours of thought which is the domain of what people like to call nothingness. This is my domain. A space-less circle in which my mind wanders and I speak to myself on the wings of a secret music. Perhaps it is not a space at all, or perhaps it is a space whose dominant is time. Ridding oneself of coordinates, one could creep away from physicality into a form of memory, a land of pure time.

And yet my thought aims at destroying memory. I aim to take time back into the marrow of nothingness through a breach in thinking. I want to be infinitely small and crawl through a hole in space, itself created via a hole in time. I seek out ditches, caverns, dimly lit grottoes where a terrifying obscurity heralds an infinite optimism and beautiful forgetting. We will talk more of the journey through the darkness to the edge of the night, to the humble acceptance of a new dawn as nothing.

There is blindness in seeing so let us close our eyes. There is too much noise, too much useless music so let us create silence. I sculpt nothingness. Non-time dances through my fingers. This is my obstinate objective, my aim and my hope. I call it freedom, although you could say that I am trapped in paradox. I know that the words I use are inadequate to express this venture, but there are no others. Accept paradox and the sky's thundering. Yes, we will get there.

Instinct guides all my movements. Improvisation is everything. My words must be bled of moments, I must write only what my emptiness allows. Thus the event speaks through me and I simultaneously free myself of what I was becoming, of what I shall never become *in fact*. The euphoria of the renting open of time itself, the passage through, out and into an outside world of wonders – my eyes can't believe what they see because believing always comes after. So it is with these movements of thought which come *as* they are written. Be patient, sometimes we need to begin at the end before discovering that the middle is infinite. Keep moving, these pages are infinite.

Massacio: Philosopher of the Eye

Paint my eyes. Fill my eyes with your eyes. Make me a believer. Let Jesus come to me and heal me. I want to rub my nose against the soil of Jerusalem. Take me to the garden of Eden.

Adam looks at Eve. Here, they are still in paradise. Their hairless bodies are innocent and they have no restraint. As such, they have no vision, not of themselves nor of any outside interference. The fruit is just inches from Eve's ominous mouth. Adam's hand resting beside her buttock sensually encourages. The snake, cherub-faced, looms above. Perfect innocence is about to disappear. They are on the verge of the catastrophic plunge into knowledge. They are about to see. As she eats the fruit, he enjoys the transgression. His enjoyment comes through looking, hers from performing. And yet, it appears, she does not enjoy. Only male looking enjoys. When they fall from Paradise, it is their eyes they cover. Knowledge comes from the eyes.

This fresco is not an image of paradise per se but the image of the end of paradise. The beginning of knowledge, knowledge through vision, through the painter's vision. Is it surprising then that painting becomes so important given the primacy of seeing? Here is the last snapshot before the fall. Could Massaccio have painted an image prior to the temptation, prior to the hesitation? Would he have had the visual repertoire, the signs to do so? A vision of pure paradise? Massacio's paintings liberate our instinctual tongue.

Peter looks down at the cripple and summons him to rise. His face is severe with concentration, with his duty. Now Peter looks up toward God with respect and fear. Because he looks up toward God to converse with him, he attains the transcendental line. Peter can look into the hearts of people and heal them because they see his faith in his eyes. His eyes which are God's eyes.

The halo-less courtesans are in conversation, eyes fixed on each other. They do not see the beggars, nor God, nor do they pay attention to what God could reveal: their hearts. They are in conversation. That is all they do. They look horizontally. Their eyes are like clothes, accompaniments to worldly business. They have invented money as God-less exchange.

Jesus has eyes, but he does not need to use them in order to see. He can direct proceedings without looking. Others look at him and take strength from the fact that he does not need to look. All gazes are upon him. He is an object of passion but his eyes are passionless. He is fulfilling a mission. He knows from the inside what he shall see, he hears what he shall see, thus he does not need to look. Eyes from in the heart. Eyes of God.

Michelangelo's <u>David</u>

Michelangelo's sculpture *David* is the male body *par excellence*. It transcends time, it transcends place. It is more Greek than Greek. This body demands to be scrutinized, it provokes. It is also a *modern* vision, because the subject is an excuse to show a lusty boy's forms. All is deception. Here, a woman to desire the male body must enter the world of the homosexual. Or is it the homosexual artist who must become a woman to create such a vision? David's *aesthetic* pose – like the figure of Bacchus holding aloft his cup of wine – is a proposition in the service of a secret desire. What allows the project to survive and triumph is Michelangelo's immense gift. Marble is the becoming god of stone and, in Michelangelo's hands, the becoming homosexual of humanity.

Silences

1.

Across the blue our sadness sends signals of light. We have been brought down by fate. Still like diamond studs in the skulls of strange birds, we shine on.

2.

I don't have words or expressions to say what I have to say, so I write reams which hint at what cannot be said – the silence. I don't write to eradicate this silence but to let it breathe, that it might speak to me again and allow me to feel its deep expression. As we know, music transforms a special form of silence which might be called loneliness. Music sends signals across the void, and often we then are as one with that void. Great sounds form a pact with silence which gives them their greatness.

3.

Thoughts press the timid cage, dancers make hybrid movements of life. The pen is liberated from the person who holds it. What is written is the pen's desire, solely the pen's desire. There is a gap between pen and eye, the gap is full of void. This gap is a bridge for the reader who fills these gaps between words. All is transitory except silence – even silence? (The writer's privilege is to allow two contrary affirmations to exist side by side, because his work can be left unfinished. Writing is a precipice overreaching silence.) Silence? Death is silence's victory? Silence is death's final comment. Does death fall in a precise moment of terrifying silence, or is it permanently present, permanently ready to claim its victim?

4.

Would it be sufficient for one person to find himself at the end of time and therefore infect all persons with the creeping inertia of timelessness? To find himself beyond death, in an infinite prism where events are withheld, where nothing ever happens ever again, where it is just a long game of waiting for life to retaliate, knowing full well that such a likelihood is nil. Has writing ever been other than a strange sense of timelessness and filling this timelessness with bizarre drawings? Surely we draw with writing.

Only at the end of time will the perfect book be written. Its writing will correspond with the end of the world and it will never be read.

Nomad Thought
Pour Gilles Deleuze

1.

The nomad teaches us this: we should not look for stable points of origin in order to reassure ourselves in our movements, but rather we should do away with the psychology which makes us dependent upon our origins and compels us to calculate our every step. We should just simply move. What we are missing is thought within movement, the ability to double movement itself, a fluid and explosive place from which to abolish the lack that origin fills, to stretch back further than origin through the weak psychology that demands the anchoring of origins. For when I think, the nomad affirms, I am not.

I am inspired in a space and time outside familiarity, in a moment that expels images of cognitive recognition. I am overtaken by an imageless moment, one of thoughtless chaos. This is the genesis of thought. With what strange forces do I communicate within this eerie state of non-being? There are thoughts which are impossible to interpret or understand, thoughts rising out of sequence. The nomad's gamble is here. Could this new thinking open onto another truer form of being? This thought is at home nowhere. The desert calls every new thinker.

The nomad thinker is at war with academic thought. He considers it to be *anti-thought*, a coward's compromise. The nomad thinker is a warrior and trains as such. He must exercise his thought in this danger zone. He must imitate the grass that grows imperceptibly *in between*. Nomad thought is ashamed of man and writes its shame.

Nomad thought is thus against the majority which is hardly surprising given the ignominious compromises philosophers have made with all species of tyrant in past decades spawning reams of dreary and supercilious commentary. What is this commentary, who is this army of commentators who cannot allow the drift, so close sometimes, it's true, to the ferment of disgraceful perversion? We must have the integrity and courage to undermine the enemy within ourselves if necessary. We must delve deeper into the molecules of fascism. Nomad thought proposes ethics to initiate the reader into the *non-fascist* life.

With this tool-box of ethics literally in hand, one can venture to places that once seemed mad. One can lose the warning signs, the detour panels, all the signifying paraphernalia of the masters of control and their strategies of prevention which stretch down into our private beings. The nomad thinker has grown sick of this regimented existence. In this world become chaos, in this proliferating fragmentation, it is no longer enough to pray for a lost unity or a new unity to come, even in some non-religious form. We must dive down into the resident multiplicity and become friends of the chaos. The nomad creates a new concept to chart this new territory of chaos and this concept is The Rhizome.

Any point of a rhizome can be connected to any other, and so it must. Everything in a rhizome is collective and functions accordingly – linguistically, biologically, economically, and politically. A rhizome forges links between meaning and power, the arts and the sciences. A mother tongue, for instance, is just a bulb which forms over subterranean roots. There are no points in a rhizome, there is only multiplicity. There are no units, only variations. The rhizome changes effortlessly from one state to another. It supposes an enlarged concept of reason, a re-defined rational within which the unthinkable and the indefinable find their place. In the beginning was *difference,* so let us repeat this difference and move with dancing feet into the nomad thinker's burrow. Look closely, this thinker is a sorcerer. Rhizome is rupture – ants and rats, drunkenness when you're in love, anger. Rhizome is lying down in a room and drawing maps of real worlds that don't exist.

2.

Thought hides what determines it. Thus thought has always had an image to which it conformed, 'an image of thought.' An image of thought is something more surreptitious than a method, less easy to identify and yet more profound, for it grounds all thought and often *despite* the thinker. An image of thought has thus always been presupposed in thinking and can be defined as *a system of coordinates, of dynamics, of orientations, as what it means to think and to orient oneself in thinking*. Hence all thought refers itself to an image of thought as a ground without which thought could not function meaningfully. For thought is not natural. Yet the philosopher has presupposed the mind as mind *and* the thinker as thinker. The philosopher wants the truth, naturally loves and desires the truth. He assumes in advance the good will of thought and all his investigations are based upon premeditated decisions, and so the search for truth would seem natural, perhaps even simple.

But what of this decision to undertake a search for truth, accepting that one possesses a method capable of overcoming the external influences which distract the mind causing it to mistake the false for the true? Would this pursuit be a matter of discovering and organizing ideas as so many explicit significations or formulations which would then assure agreement in a grand parliament of logical minds? Within such a conception of thought – that is, supposedly having found a universal method – error is necessarily the trap. Such a method would have to enable the thinker to discover how to neutralize the diversions which impede the thinker from thinking, namely the passions and sensations; the body which leads the thinker away from the truth and into error. Only once these annoying anti-truths have been injected with the vaccine of correct method can thought proceed and the world become known to us through a book which would be a mirror of the outside world representing it as it is.

Raising an ominous finger, the nomad thinker says, "What if these bodily affects suppressed by your dreary classical method were really the very forces that motivate your logical thought? How then could your desire for truth be a natural property of thought, for thought itself would then be derived from that which is *anti-natural*."

The nomad thinker further interrogates the sedentary philosopher: "Pray, why is it you seek the truth so stubbornly? Why is it you consider the body to be synonymous with the irrational and error? Who is it you serve so secretly with your thought? Whose power are you grounding? Who are you thereby excluding with your natural dominion over the truth?"

3.

There is no truth, that before being truth, is not the bringing into effect of a sense or the realization of a value. Everything depends on the value and sense of what we think. We always have the truths we deserve as a function of the sense of what we conceive and the value of what we believe.

Age-old definitions of truth and orthodox methods of discovery are then wholly undetermined and dependent upon something outside thought *appropriating it and making it true*. So truth-seekers have witnessed their activity falling into disrepute. They have seen their efforts placed at the helm of murderous regimes. They have seen their idols pillaged and looted, and they have found themselves falling with their idols. Now they have named this state of falling idols, they call it *chaos*. They say we live in a hellish world without definition or method, without thought or truth.

The nomad thinker asks: Who is profiting from this chaos, what are the forces behind it, and who are the new masters who impose simplistic answers with a society of spectacle like a glitzy screen over the terrifying realities of our day? His answer: The masters of universal capitalism. The nomad thinker will never cease to pose the question: Who do your truths serve, who profits from your thinking? Why is your thought so easily appropriated by the dominant Powers? Thought must be understood and evaluated according to the forces of power that determine us to think, and to think this rather than that.

Nomads have been persecuted since time immemorial. They know there will always be a thinker to help the state control its population, to gently exterminate its opposition. But how can one create a new conception of thought itself? How shall this new image of thought be created – for it will be an eternal creation, an infinite movement – if it must plunge into the unconscious of the thinker to allow the forces of the body to play? This new image of thought is a *rhizome* and not a tree, a multitude of lines rather than a path from one point to another. How must it be practiced and written if it must always be wary of becoming appropriated by all forms of state apparatuses, parodists, and lazy hedonists? Why is it that, finally, in chaos there might be a thought, a real thought born in the lines of the un-thought?

We are not yet thinking. We are still waiting to liberate thought from its prison. But can such thought exist whilst mistrusting its every step? Does such thought not lead to myriad new errors and illusions? Is this not a new idealism? Are the body and the passions as dangerous as the logical mind? Do we not risk falling into thoughtless perversion and thereby recalling the great biblical prophecies?

Man shall be multiplied as he seizes upon the forces capable of making thought something active, the power capable of making it an affirmation.

4.

Thought is by no means the natural exercise of a faculty. It shall first be necessary to do violence to thought, to this old weary thought we employ despite ourselves. There must be some event which forces thought to become active. There has to be some necessity there that forces its way into thought, something unknown which begets the known. A violence undergone by thought in thought, a process, a becoming, a journey which becomes thought as it tries to think. So there must be an event – a violent event – which brings the thinker back together after having dispelled him and his thinking, an event which drags up the signs and the blood and the liquid colours of the unconscious. For thought is not won without effort and pain. *The whole unconscious of the thinker must be brought into play*.

The classical image of thought is nothing more than a dogmatic repression of real thought. It is a trap for the sinews of invention. It says: I think therefore I am. But to *think* is to move underneath who I am and become something else. *I become therefore I think*. Kafka could have gone further but he got scared. It was the classical image of control – his father's power – that sent panic signals to his brain and body. Truth is not given to us when we know who we are, nor does it sit conveniently waiting for us up in some ideal sky. We produce truth by constructing a machine for interpreting the world. But we go further than interpreting, we throw our whole body of sensations at the things we analyze and our work becomes the ephemeral and infinite event of that analysis. Thus our sensations merge with the object analyzed. A painter produces an apple, he does not copy one. The painting is the very sensation of the apple which does not exist in the apple as such unless it is captured by the body-eye-brush of the painter.

The spider is a cruel insect. When he writes a novel, he eliminates many characters in the search for truth. Why? Because they are false images. They are illusions, mirages in the desert. He analyzes them, but as symptoms, and then spits them out. Flies, on the other hand, agree too often and are always carrying on unutterably boring conversations with their friends, likewise reaching agreements in public they don't hold to in private. They all think the same way because they have all been taught to think the same way, and they are convinced there is only one way to think, and that it is all inscribed in certain canonical books of which one is of course totally ignorant. Hence they can ejaculate: How can you possibly draw such a conclusion if you haven't read so and so?! They believe all sane individuals act of their own free will and are guided by an implacable intelligence. They condemn any contrary viewpoint. Simply put: they are an elite who observe things from a distance and subscribe to laws which they call truths. The spider does not care much for these high class flies who flit about with *their* intelligence. He knows that intelligence does not *precede* thought. Real thought is dangerous for flies, that's why the spider can trap them so easily. Plato, the Greek spider, spoke of *a disjunctive or involuntary use of the faculties whereby the sensuous qualities of things could be grasped by a remembering soul.* This 'remembering soul' would then interpret the quality of things to discover their meaning. And yet, for Plato the mood for love always referred to a pre-existent idea of loving which this particular mood was imitating. Therefore it was the goal of such involuntary memory to recover the pre-existent essence of love. For the modern spider, *the slanting ray of the setting sun, an odour or a flavour or a draft, all such ephemeral qualitative complexes, as they are termed, are evaluated through the sensations they stimulate and which penetrate the subject. They cause an event in the spider's body and set off a chain of subjective associations which we are not free to experiment with the first time we experience them, they are too strong for us, too painful, too good. We can't yet bring them home to our intelligence. They are involuntary.*

This involuntary and subjective aspect is, however, merely primary and beckons to an essence which would no longer be an *idea* as in Plato, but rather an aesthetic viewpoint or superior reality – a plateau of free air – which is unravelled as it were from the experience of the sign which caused the initial subjective shock. *The important thing is that the viewpoint transcends the individual no less than the essence transcends the mood.* The modern spider's state of soul remains inferior to the viewpoint it creates in the web. In fact the web is nothing other than a thousand viewpoints – contradictory perhaps, but that's the essence. The viewpoint has to be attained through a journey in sensations. Those that go the same way can guarantee a certain surprising community of sense. The narrator-spider is a modern insect. His theory of essences fragments outside reality into a series of discontinuous viewpoints, accepting that different individuals can run the gamut of sensations to arrive at similar plateaus. Totality is nevertheless shattered. Amid the shards, amid this multiplicity of parts without whole, only the signifying structure of the work of art can guarantee any truth or objectivity. Nor can subjectivity, shattered by involuntary emotion across time, remain stable or identical to itself in time. The subject has become subjective process. The role of memory must also change as it ceases to serve a synthetic intelligence which directs the mind toward the world and toward its reproduction in the mirror of representation. The spider's memory itself is a factory for acts of memory production.

There is no fixed method which can make us think correctly and it is in fact very doubtful if thinking correctly is actually desirable. Method is thus a question of strategy and is contingent upon the event which engenders the necessity for thinking. Sensations are not the path to error but the signs of a new intelligence, the body.

The eternal truth of the event is grasped only if the event is also inscribed in the flesh.

THREE

Colours

Now the lemons are in flower,
the almonds too.
The wisteria cascades
by the bleached walls
and the vines knit
a shelter from the sun.
I become white and
mauve and yellow.
I want to go further now,
I want to go beyond you,
beyond this harmony of solitudes.
My heart opens to these colours,
to the ecstasy of spring,
whether you are here
or whether you are not.
Nature's feast carries me away
upon the waves to the white cliffs,
to the ancient civilization
on the top of the hill.
I can hear the most infinite of echoes
as my heart opens to blue dawn.
I know you will come
and meet me here.

Funeral

You hugged a dream since you were born. You believed death was something beautiful, a realm into which you could slide and drop blissfully free of pain. Death was a hope, a liberation and you dreamt of it often.

Your hand outstretched from the heart grabs at an object to stop you from falling into the mad coffin of hell. You can reach out your hand, you can stretch out your arm, but the walls are crumbling. Now you suffer too much, perhaps I am a part.

I sat for years against that falling wall, I will carry the scars and the hurt. There was a time when you broke everything and you came hunting for me. Your tears flowed incessantly, your arms rose and then dropped pathetically to your side.

Now you look out for the last hope, of dying and leaving us all to guilt. You shout and swear and utter aphorisms of hatred. I have learnt to accept your hatred, I have learnt to let the wall come down. Death cannot save you from madness, it cannot stop the fall.

You look over the dead one, the cold one. You touch his face which could have been yours, you love his eyes which could have been yours. Your heart bleeds fiercesome tears which should have been ours. The free melodies of death will have to wait before their tender hands caress your cold skull.

Autumn Leaves

1.

You asked for writing. How much I would love to drape my writing around you, leaves of books sketched upon your thighs and stomach. I look for your movement, but you are still. Your eyes hide a forbidden tale of ecstatic intuition, and the decision to eradicate its source. I did have dreams, dreams of you as I acquiesced to my erasure. I was that event in the past that never happened nor could ever be realised in the future. With every measure, you imbibe an ounce of forgetting. You look at me, suddenly, with a hardness born of hidden preoccupations. I assure you, I no longer exist nor ever existed. I have no ardour, I have no passion. I am a dream unto myself. I write, and when I write I am unaware of the importance of reality. Now that I can't write, I am certain of not existing. I am a bird that has long since taken flight. You are my stories, and I shall remain in love whilst you have forgotten me. You can become music.

My nails dig into walls
for the secret of you,
I have the taste in my mouth
of a wolf who has licked
the wound of an escaped prey.

2.

Five long years. Calculations replaced dancing. Arithmetic replaced learning. I sold my soul to the dream in the street. I ran around with merchants and gangsters. I fell foul of the book. I added up wads of notes and took them all to the casino. I sold paintings for barrels of liquor. I found a vision of hard despair. I lost you divine Literature, lost you in this mayhem of violence where I battled to win. To win what? More of the same, more of this carnal repetition of exchange. I lost you for five long years. My inner voice, my love beyond loves, you who cannot be surrendered.

It is hard to be forgiving with myself when I have been as harsh as I have and yet this eager sound tells me my true nature has not suffered. I was born to carry this sound! So, dear page's concert, save me from the forceps of indifference and let love unfold the true feelings in my heart, even if *she* does not dare follow the foray this far. I must take it that the very act of drawing these affects suffices to mystify your heart.

3.

I would take your world and send vibrations through it until exhaustion trembled. I would fasten your blue gaze to mine for a long season in Paradise. I would create great movements between us just as I covered over their every trace. I would surrender my body to the unadulterated possibilities of caress. We would whisper to each other through the night until our embers were reduced to a timid grey. I see you from the other bank, we are separated by the current, and yet the current is ours alone. I know you feel as I do, knowing also that we must return to our routine and remember how to lie.

There would be no reward but the prolonged holiday we would create for ourselves under the warm rays of the vocabulary we would send across our bodies. But what bodies are these, you ask, where words make inroads through the flesh and murmurs wander labyrinths of improvised desires? My eyes look at yours and every moment is pierced with expectation. I meditate in your eyes and your laughter frees me. Now I can't take my eyes from your, I can't take my laughter from your mouth. I want to go inside to be with you, as my eyes think of your eyes.

4.

Words fill the white pastures of this page as I lament the impossibility of touching you, words which form themselves into lines which are the strictest equivalent of desire. Lines which rather than be stifled overflow and colour this notebook. Why did heaven send me your eyes, to make a mockery of my seriousness? I sing to myself in your gaze.

Our voices express a love our bodies rarely repay, as our bodies rarely carry the courage of our convictions. Hence we must surrender to the poem which is a tightrope over the abyss into which we dare not dive. I'll take your hand, I'll call you across. I'll show you the promised land. I should like to invent a world where joy did not give way to despair, where our hopes did not flounder in gloom, where we might keep apace with excitement and worry not, for all would go well and of its own accord. As we wouldn't know the meaning of disappointment, we wouldn't hate, or crave revenge. We would be at play with ourselves as laughter enveloped our minds.

Cool autumn leaves,
beeze under clothing,
hands clutching at hope,
pain of rejection,
desire knows no hurdle.

5.

Let others come and go, here you are by my side even now that you've gone. You were a permanent conversation, you were *you*. Your voice oscillated between the crisp authority of your mother and the resigned submissiveness and sweetness of your father. You ran from one to other, schizophrenic desire. Your body is a chord strung between embrace and despair, hope and rejection, kindness and totalitarian impatience. Yet your eye is pure, even as truth flows from despair. You accept your body but you do not seek it out, nor do you crave to be touched. You are a white statue rising from the slab yet returning when your day's work is done. I eat away at the stone with my teeth, my lips ache, my tongue seeks your lips. You are naked, I have you in my hands. I stand you up, I lie you down. I comb your hair, I perfume your body. Your thoughts are free to roam the room. I capture your expression in an instant, I see the beginnings of a smile.

6.

I look for poems in this devilish grey maze of a city. I inhale fumes from the big red buses as they pass. I finish a Barolo and a pizza. I kiss you still, three days later. Even the wine cannot outlast your taste! I look for poems in the bustle of the streets. I look at bare tree tops and leaves trodden in the mush. Cold clouds break over me. I walk miles by day and by night. I have crossed an infinity of streets. I write poems in my head to the tune of my steps, as my steps delve for this secret flowering. I look in vain for you here, yet this is where you are. I read Holderlin's *Diotima* and cry fat tears. I can feel your breath mingling with the autumn, but our love must be a symphony, the effulgence of spring.

7.

Lying with clouds of cigar smoke sending my head round the walls of this prison, Stochelo's guitar liberates me. In one fell swoop, with one grand ricochet of his staccato gypsy strings, I am free. I inhale this music through the heart, I hear hidden secrets in his guitar. I understand his voice. Your song I have yet to grasp. I do not know what you like or dislike, because you are too polite, the fruit of your education.

I wake up with this pen in my hand. Forbidden thoughts moaning in my head, I set to work without food or drink I look hard at the white page, but the incessant murmur of traffic disgusts me, and the great tree outside this third-floor flat leers as it looms as if to say: You're just as responsible as any other! Although these words are jumbled, I am amazed to see the pen move so fast. Yesterday, I thought I was going, crushed by the weight of impossibility, but today there is something optimistic battering at the gate.

*Your fingers open
an oasis of silver water.
Branches dip into
the pool where you swim.*

Petit Poème en Français

Tu ne danses plus pour moi depuis longtemps.
Je cherche ta silhouette dans la nuit. Pourtant tes yeux rejettent toute douceur. Le vent ayant tourné. Et je suis surpris de voir surgir la Mort. Je meurs encore de mourir. Mais tu dors si paisiblement comme un enfant à coté de ton enfant. Le visage de l'une tournée vers le visage de l'autre, les bras entrelacés d'amour.

J'envoie donc un poème à travers le lit. J'ouvre ta tête et je poste mes mots. Je contourne ton œil vert-gris. Personne n'entend le papier tomber, seulement le poète mort, celui qui enregistre tout depuis le départ et qui écrit sa passion dans tous les détails.

Je te connais poète, je connais ta haine
et je connais ton amour. Je te connais danseuse.
Je connais ton pas de traître, je connais tes vagues
et ta marée.

J'attends devant une page comme un musicien
devant sa partition blanche qui verrait danser
ses notes entre elles.
Je suis seul dans cette nuit pour toujours.
Je n'ai plus peur de rien ni de toi ni des autres.
Je suis à même le silence, à même le vol
et le cri des oiseaux.
Je suis à même l'eau, à même le torrent,
à même la boue au sol.
Je suis terre. Je suis le masque même de la graine qui s'éclot et qui meure au rayon de la première aurore.

Je te connais poète, je connais ta haine
et je connais ton amour. Je te connais danseuse.
Je connais ton pas de traître, je connais tes vagues
et ta marée.

Rien ne peut m'enlever le bonheur
de tes hanches.
Rien ne peut assassiner
les lignes désespérées de ton cœur.
Même aujourd'hui le jour où je meurs.
Ta haine t'a perdu comme tu me perds
ce jour pour me retrouver – qui sait? –
un autre encore.
Je porterai ta fille du haut
de mes deux mains
Je l'aimerai comme je t'aimais
comme j'aimerai encore.

Je te connais poète, je connais ta haine
et je connais ton amour. Je te connais danseuse.
Je connais ton pas de traître, je connais tes vagues
et ta marée.

<u>A Shy Libertine</u>

1.

Every path is a sketch of moments. I have stolen desires in my heart. I move from relationship to relationship, leaving behind a sum of breakage, of tears, of anger and pain. I cannot do otherwise, it is my body that orders me. And yet nothing stops me from starting all over again, from lighting another fire, from effacing a thousand stolen desires for a new genuine hope at real love.

Territories define most people. Here they can live, there they can't. When they are at home they can speak a certain type of language. Elsewhere they are mute. I move along invisible lines. I am a stranger everywhere hence I am at home on the road and I can assure you that I move, I sneak past the gateposts and live in the intervals, in the free spaces between prisons. I escape definitions.

Once in a while, a moment falls, a living possible moment. I see you in the terror trenches, in the paucity where meaning vanishes and discrimination mounts. I see my own tears rise from my eyes and dance. I see your face. I see the child you were and I loved. I see you and feel you. I feel you in my arms and wonder how I ever took to the road again.

But a moment will come, a woman dressed and ready to spill herself in words. I will be able to see again, hear again and stop for a fraction and feel. A flower can blossom from the tarmac. Love in the global ghetto is possible.

Think then of a voice, neither mine nor yours, a voice generated by the book itself. A voice born of a thousand voices. Born of events transformed into writing. From the blank mind I rise as the page before the writer. My voice is made solely of silken moments, an improvisation from the cosmos. Words are arrows thrown across the void. I must try and put them together as best I can.

I sit before my kiln. Everything seems artificial. I have come to mould, to mould you as best I can and leave our love to chance's beautiful hand. Hence I beg you to become a simulated crafted object greater than its original in poor visual reality. I strive for a further dimension where you can make me write. From the deep, stirs another eye.

How is a poem born? You must help me. You must learn to love and you will know. How many tears must fall, held in their falling? How many hopes dashed, how many fertile encounters? The young man must cut loose and separate himself from himself, take what is from what isn't and land his soul on the table of chance. He must learn to repeat the effortless effort.

Snow mounted guard before your prison gates. I came to warm you and set the thaw in motion to escape the ice. Negation can be negated. Snow melts and you begin to sing. Why so many prisons from new freedoms? I wonder if the first principle of freedom is to learn to not exist, lessons in non-being. I distil metaphysics of black night. Ecstasy tunes. Hell and paradise both. Ascension. Journal of the Wanderer. *Trust no more in man, he has but breath in his nostrils*. It is time now to travel back through time once more, to the winter alps through myriad repeated horizons, through a thousand processed paintings.

Freeze frame. The characters: protagonist, the writer (lover in the first person), Miss C. from Jamaica, Emily Dickinson, a suitcase full of books.

He writes:

"Every morning, inventing new horizons, living this eternal present of books and events born of fine encounters, entering the relations that govern books, crossing boundaries into forbidden musings, becoming *other* in the pages of my sole luggage – books.

Is today's horizon, as midday sounds from the *clocher* in the village, the pink sky where Emily's moonlit lines rise? Lines waiting for the intrepid idler who might sleep over their way?

There are liquid mirrors on the tarmac, tears of ice glisten there and wink up at me as I wander. My beige overcoat slung over my left arm, right thumb raised at the passing cars. The southern wind plies the wheat and the jagged snow caps write the Swiss horizon's indifference. My suitcase full of books weighs heavy but I dance gaily by the waysides. Nothing but books? Not quite. A few changes of clothes, a silk tie my ex-fiancée Rebecca had bought me long ago, toothbrush and razor, antique typewriter. I take many of the books with me as company. I may not read them all. Some are there just to give me moral support. Memories of good friends now that I have abandoned all ties to the past. Zarathustra for instance has been with me now for five years solid. *Philosophy in the Boudoir. The Book of Questions. The Book of Disquietude. Paradis.*

2.

The world isn't so bad. I'm buoyed up with this strange and eager energy, some faith somewhere that it's going to turn out right as I adventure into this unknown orgy. So many cars just pass on by, not even so much as looking, others dissect you as they pass, looking hard at your presence, there, odd, by the wayside, seemingly content to be alone in the bright chill. Ah, when can we start looking really at each other again? Really! Without this terror, this mistrust and envy? Sure, we have lost the collective bond that binds us together but do we need to constantly do each other down? Setting one challenger against another? If he's not doing well, then someone can take advantage of the vacant space he leaves behind. Can competition be a collective hope? Better to drop into chaos, that's my wager. Drop, drop, forget the imperatives, drop, live on the sidelines, at least for a while, the better to discover some truths.

One can paint two types of contemporary nihilist. On the one hand, those pessimists about everything; and on the other, those optimists about nothing. The former stays at home. He is the perfect cynic. He knows all is rotten but reckons there can be nothing doing, better to make do with little, have one's pleasures the best one can, and comment wittily on the eternal failures of those who hope. The other, the optimist about nothing, makes an impossible and absurd wager. He's come to similar conclusions, but reckons there's a force worth following and practising. He has greater faith in the body. He can't help it he's got the affirmative marrow, perhaps perversely. He gives the benefit of the doubt. He's probably less well educated, too. He likes to loosen ties and gets on fine all by himself. He's not afraid of being different, not even of going mad. He lives his life like some kind of sublime sickness. He knows suffering and is fond of the desert and the parched Mediterranean bush. He believes the world is still a fascinating place. Simply put: he has faith that escape is possible. And he proves it, day and night. He's definitely not as correct a writer as the former.

The pessimist believes in rules and lives by them and none are more sacred than the laws of grammar! Oh damned positivists! On the contrary, the optimist about nothing has forgotten so much, it is from the depth of his amnesia that he scribbles away day after day, rarely knowing where he's headed some evenings. He gets lost only to find himself again. He makes mistakes. He lives the hour where midday can become midnight. He is intent on achieving sleepless bliss. He can be awkward, brash and yet his lines have an assurance about them beyond the person who wrote them and which stem from the point of non-self which his amnesia has allowed him to reach. This is the point, impersonal point which gives him certainty. And yet now he knows how the writing will always get the better of him: the price he'll have to pay for prophecy. *Tout est paradis dans cet enfer, on y revient!*

The car came from over the hill, I heard it skid that's for sure, but then there was a blank, a suspended moment. Her hand was outstretched and I saw her elegant smile look down at me. I was bleeding I think, not much though, and I stretched out my hand and we touched. 'I'm so terribly sorry,' she said, and we just kept looking at each other in the eyes, something saying yes from both sides. Then I fell faint.

Her voice was of a pure English aristocratic, her smile broad and charming to the full, but the sun was blinding and my eyes closed under the brightness. Later she would say: 'I felt something supernatural overwhelm me, it was too strong for me. It wasn't because I knocked you down, because you were really fine. But the accident was so bizarre, I felt I had to take you home. And your face seemed different to me, there was something about it, I couldn't resist.'

"Is Bliss then, such Abyss,
I must not put my foot amiss
For fear I spoil my shoe?

I'd rather suit my foot
Than save my boot –
For yet to buy another pair
Is possible,
At any store.

But Bliss, is sold just once.
The Patent lost,
None buy it anymore.
Say, Foot, decide the point –
The Lady cross, or not?
Verdict for Boot!"

3.

The sun descends over the silver caps once more, shadows lengthen and creep along the walls of houses where shutters hastily close on night's glacial winds. I whisper over Miss C.'s dark long dry hair: she's almost asleep, in that seductive half-slumber where subversion often triumphs so devilishly!

I'm feeling better already. Miss C. installed me in her red satin sheets only a week ago. She had brought me beer and recited Shakespeare to me as I slumbered deliriously a few hours. I think she'd forgive me if I said she was a fascinating subject. A tall, beautiful black lady from the Caribbean of working class parents – her father was a bus conductor in London brought over to fill the employment shortage in the sixties. Miss C. was born in Jamaica and came to England when she was five. Her father soon lost his job and went back to Kingston. She has only seen him twice in the last fifteen years. Her mother had several lovers, perhaps one of them was her real father. She doubts her paternal heritage. She was bent on success. She studied hard, very hard, and quickly made it to University where she studied Science. She passed her exams with honours and got a job with an international organisation in Geneva. She claimed to be fighting *fascisms* all over the world. A success story I suppose which might explain her thoroughly optimistic soul. She believes we are heading toward a new re-evaluation of values, a new *Lumières*, where a new form of knowledge will prevail, enabling us to overcome our old binary wars and mistakes. Plurality is her favourite term. We must learn to think in the plural, she says. Her enunciation of Shakespeare is fantastic, and from memory too!

Imagine Miss C. coming out of the jacuzzi, a towel gently slipped round her firm ripe buttocks. She speaks the following lines straight at the camera just as the most perfect toffee English rose might and she loves every word of it, just as she loves every pore of her skin and every molecule of her sensuality:

"Our revels now are ended. These our actors,
As I foretold you, were all spirits and
Are melted into air, into thin air:

And, like the baseless fabric of this vision,
The cloud-capp'd towers, the gorgeous palaces,
The solemn temples, the great globe itself,
Yea, all which it inherit, shall dissolve
And, like this insubstantial pageant faded,
Leave not a rack behind. We are such stuff
As dreams are made on, and our little life
Is rounded with a sleep."

For Miss C., poetry is the greatest human act possible. A divine revelation! A supernatural offering! The poet is a celestial being, nothing of the human about him. Quite so. At least almost nothing. Just enough of the human, if you see what I mean. Whoever said I was lucky? It was her, my temporary friend, my passage through the Swiss Alps who christened me. 'You are a strange mix. You are a shy libertine.' Coming from such a perfect person, I could only agree.

So here I am now finally at the cherished point where I have nothing to do, the point where I can make things happen, events occur. Miss C. is my present event. She is kind. She is as beautiful as can be and has a devastatingly athletic body with the kind of behind that makes me go literally crazy. What's more she has just finished an affair with an uptight American scientist who wasn't up to it as regards bedly matters. He had the apparently common white boy complex. Miss C. was charmed to behold that I did not suffer the same complaint. Needless to say, Europeans have yet to suffer the battering assaults of the new Cultural Revolution which hails from left wing universities and which hangs heavily on the consciousness of the impressionable American television youth. I remember my three years spent over there at New York University. I often had to lock myself away to laugh. But I had the good sense and traitorous nature to go along with most of what was said, seeking out the underground racism, ousting the signifying enemy from the vile texts of phallocratic men, assailing macho male bodies with invective. With Miss C., I let idleness overwhelm me. What joy to lie naked in these foreign sheets late into the night with her reciting Emily Dickinson, letting chance guide me night after night. Miss C. you are Miss Chance. The world is bad but we get on anyhow. Society stinks but we find ways to circumvent her vicious equalizing mathematics, her ploys from The Outside.

4.

Accepting the above, we wallow for years in the most acute difficulties. Escape is not something simple like finding a key and opening a secret padlock. Escape is prepared underground for ages before the simple actions can be performed in the free paddock of open oxygens. Early on, you accept the inability to lie, to sign on the dotted line, to accept orders from cretins, to pay taxes in order to line the pockets of hordes of vengeful slobs, to say thank you when your benefactor wishes to do you in, to take a fall and say you're a wimp, to admit you're wrong when you're right, to pass yourself off as a fool. No! The air-conditioned nightmare is not for us! No! Whence our permanent exclusion. The impossibility of being recognized. The manifold attempts to make you fail and then to pinpoint your failure as an example for future generations! No thank you!

Imagine this body then. The body of the shy libertine. Coffee, eyes opening, brain dull, notebook, red ink, pen dancing as if night continued into day, the thread intact still. The pen is a sleepy interlude of night in day. He remembers: *to write is to sleep a deeper slumber, to be dead*. Or: *slumber is the slow analysis of sensations*. Or again: *to sail is what's necessary, not to reach a port*. Or even: *the written word is the only tolerable form of communication, as it isn't a stone in a bridge between souls but a ray of light between stars*. Or one of his favourites: *one must have chaos in one to give birth to a dancing star*. Yes, yes. How many of us care to listen to ourselves speak, even into our unconscious speakings? And what if they began to? They would assuredly be led to open the unconscious gates, the gates which most pragmatically keep us from our own chaos. To write is to forge the singular machine which lets out the unconscious flood and processes it, turning negative into positive, sublimating it as it were. To write is to occupy that fine interval between the conscious and the unconscious. So it is the pen which guides the mind, which veritably reads life, makes sense of it. It is with the pen that we read, that we dip, duck and dive, weave, bob and thrive.

Into all of this we move, tracing our lines, books, conversations, traumas. Is there anywhere we cannot go? Are their still regions unturned or censored? Do we have to be politically answerable for our every word when the unconscious has no love of such prudish filters? What should we avoid writing about to please Society's acolytes? I am answerable to another ledger. Fingers ride the keys of a deeper night, of another time. Books have put an end to the illusion of linearity. The writer is slowly lowered on a thread and then suddenly there is speed all about, entering the body. Yet the rope is strong and slows it down. All is movement, all is real. Take on your unconscious warriors! Challenge the chaos! Take up your dice! Become a body of dice! Throw your own body into the struggle! Enough of insides and outsides, closets and dirty little secrets! Become a fucking secret yourself! Sound the bugles of your unconscious song! Expand the conscious! This is reason, not the terrifying irrational! We are living an unprecedented expansion of the rational, else a new barbarism! Enough archaic cults! Exorcise your demons, your deliriums! Interpret your dreams! Burst through your screens, your mirror fantasies, your bondage trips! Tell your tale of the new non-fascist power and reason! Become optimists, even if you believe in nothing! Optimists about nothing! Be passionate in despair! Show us your true colours! Create your desires! Let's hear your dance, your shooting stars, your dancing planets! Onward new courageous ones!

Miss C.: Why not say we can be optimistic in the large and pessimistic in the small. I mean, naturally there is no reason why an Arab and a Jew, a white and a black, should not get on perfectly well – we're all humans.

I reply: I think one should be optimistic in the small and pessimistic in the large. There is no good society possible, hence the problem of trying to do away with religion through revolution: you always end up reproducing it somewhere else. And yet there is a necessary eruption of the unexpected, perceived as new, when it is simply the repetition of something as yet to be deciphered, understood. Which is why you have to fight for a certain continuity in the large and yet fight for the singularly unexpected in the small.

My relationship with beautiful Miss C. ended in the same manner it had begun – unexpectedly. One morning we began to argue. It was about a month since she had picked me up from the roadside. I looked at her and asked if she thought it was time for me to leave. She didn't say yes or no but her face was sad. I packed my books and my sundry possessions into my bag and kissed her goodbye. We didn't exchange numbers – this was before emails and mobile phones. A month had seemed such long time, and yet we hadn't managed a tear. Perhaps, each in our own way, we had both cried afterwards, secretly hoping we would see each other again."

If You Seek a Path

If you seek a path to yourself, tread on me. If you should need to shed your shackles, come give me your key. Have you ever heard nothing breathe? I'll show you the way: walk across my back, climb into my arms, hold me tight, hold me sweet, don't let me sleep. Open yourself to my lips, sip from my fountain, and I'll speak in your tongue.

Forms of Paradise

I became invisible a long time ago. I forgot the rain and I forgot the cold. I saw blue sky pouring, and I came to drink at the well. I rose at dawn and at dusk. I placed sunsets in my suitcase and counted the clouds between yesterday and the morning I would see you. Far-off lands became familiar to me. I communicated with the ghosts of poets. I carried the sweetest memories and forgot all that could do me down. I became a mountain to shelter you in pain. I learned to stretch high but I also learned to lay low when the murderers of happiness came to town, the ones who take possession and call us theirs, the ones who stamp our fists with syllables of intolerance. I wrote you poems when they stole all my belongings and sent me to jail, the same day they killed the young student in the marketplace with a deft kick to the temple. Your tears drowned your cheeks. Each dream has its nightmare, and despite our young age we were already experimenting with forms of paradise.

Heartbeat Still

Your eyes, summersaults on the breeze. You lick with your eyelashes, your face rises loud and sings. You pull dreams from my body, and lay a carpet of roses on my flesh, and still I cannot say *yes*. From my dumb teeth chatter prophecies of despair.

I dreamt of peace, of your hands clasped around mine in the night. I felt your whole body in my hand. You had already said *yes* when we met, when you spied me from a distance of blue incandescent heat and vodka rising.

I speak better in silence, sowing in the white furrows. I would like to learn to fly on the back of my poems to your warm bedside, where I needn't be nor become, but rest and lie with my heartbeat still.

Wild Palms

I remember the Professor one day slipping me a Faulkner novel. Nothing he ever did was innocent. A story of adultery – a piece of history. They'll look back on it in years to come and say Faulkner was the one who best understood those hard times. Fiction! There's never been a more ridiculous term! False for them maybe, written in a language they call lies, but truth, assuredly truth: *Le mensonge qui dit la Bien sur et pour toujours jusqu'à votre mort pauvres têtes molles d'humanité pourrie!*

The future lovers meet at a party in this so-called story. She's married and the first time she is approached by her future lover she says 'no no don't touch me' and rushes down the stairs into the safety of the street and into a cab, which passes along a long avenue, now secure in knowing that she has yet to commit *the sin* and can proudly tell her husband: 'No no, nothing happened.' She doesn't yet have to lie. She wants the adultery so badly but fights against it because it *is* a sin. This is the historical fact. Fifty years ago, sin existed. Sin felt within bones and blood and pulse. Is it still? Does it send adrenalin the same way? (Think of the Balzac heroine going into a convent to avoid committing adultery.)
No, today a sense of sin has become an ideology. It is no longer felt within the body. Ladies can't go into a trance to rid themselves of the seizure of sexual desire. Its corollary is true: how can they enjoy sin itself to the full, to the borders of death? They can't. Today, sin is a dogma imposed upon the individual by repressive politics, just as marrying *or* committing adultery has become a question

of human pride. It is no longer felt within the body. In fact, the question begs: *what is still felt within the body?*

But surprise surprise! – the protagonist returns to find the languishing wife. She has been calling to him in silence through the locked windows of her husband's prison. Implacable destiny! And the narrator notes that her husband hands the suitor his wife in an almost identical ritual to the conventional mumbo jumbo of father and bride at a wedding. Why? Because he wants rid of her? He has other business to attend to, an adultery of his own to pursue? Or is there something that impedes him from loving his wife? Or does he secretly wish to witness the adultery? These pages are full of subtle and covert insinuations. In any case, the future lovers are at a crossroads and the protagonist has the following thoughts: *'You are born, submerged in anonymous lockstep with the teeming anonymous myriad of your time and generation; you get out of step once, falter once, and you are trampled to death.'*

What makes you take the plunge? Does Fate's hand push you, as if suddenly you are no longer a spectator? This is your story and you are writing it – paragraph by paragraph – with your blood and your tears, with your very nerve-ends! (I took that step out of line a long time ago and I'm still fighting.) The narrator in the novel considers love to be vanquished. At this point on the crossroads, he has come to the conclusion that love is contrary to society, that love is not love at all but a convenient illusion.

They have got rid of love just as they destroyed art, just as they got rid of Christ and now all we have is the ubiquitous (impersonal and senseless) whir of technology in the place of God's infinite image and voice.

Mother

Born of love,
I was born of love,
of a love loved.
I was born of being loved,
with love-words
pronounced over me,
with your eyes
fixed upon me,
with the hurt I had already
inflicted upon you.

Born into love
into the ocean of love,
cleansed of deadly knowledge.
Born of your loves loved,
I felt your eyes dim
and fall away into dusk.
I never heard a scream
nor a cough,
never saw a tear fall
nor your head sway
with inner fear.
I was love, my name love.

You look at me
with love.
You look at my words now
with love,
wondering how I managed to
escape you,
how love could have
escaped love.

The Source

Have you heard tides rise inside you? Waves crash in your heart? Have you ever cried for falling chestnuts or oaks losing their leaves in a gale? A thousand invisible tides overwhelm me. And yet I cannot name this feeling. I need to stretch out a hand. I need to hear a song. I need to feel the difference between one tear and her sister? I need to redefine subtleties. This is where I find you in the glow of constantly changing colours. A leaf rusts and golden it waits, then falls to the infinite humus where music serenades its gentle demise. I sit and listen.

I dived into the source, to live before feeling becomes feeling, before breathing ruins our animal thought. I want to live in a space which precedes sentiment. I want to sing where no one has sung before. I want the stillness of the winds. I want the beauty of pre-human silence. It is a question of running away, don't they say? Of banishment, of exile? Yes, but these are not easy paths when your body must learn to die and live again on the frontiers, the precipitous edge of its potential.

You are my teacher. You banished violence from your life. You loved with every sound until the songs flocked to your side. You are the tiniest wisp of white hope stretching across the deep blue of the Southern sky and soon we shall become simply blue.

The Sun in My Heart

The sun in my heart
will burn the rain
from the skies.
Your smile of sweetness
running round my soul
laughs at the thought
of taking a dip
in the well of love.